Ryan Farquhar (Harker Kawasaki) leads
Keith Amor (Craig Honda) over Hanlon's Leap
in the Open race, Kells, July 2008

between the hedges

a celebration of 40 years of road racing

Stephen Davison

BLACKSTAFF
PRESS

BELFAST

John Burrows (McAdoo Kawasaki),
Cookstown 100, April 2003

Covering the ground

Although I have known Clifford McLean for over a decade it wasn't until we sat down together to work on this book that we realised that we had both taken our first photographs of Irish road racing at the same place – Cloughwater Church on the old Mid-Antrim 150 course. Twenty years apart, we had both poked our lenses through the railings to capture the action as the bikes passed the churchyard.

Born in 1942, Clifford had a head start on me. A sixties child, I shared with him the same County Antrim roots and a family history of involvement in motorbike racing. The roads around our home areas of Ballymoney and Tardree were instilled with a love of two-wheel sport and fathers and uncles guided us through the paddock gate. An interest in recording the spectacular sights that we watched from the hedgerows enticed us to buy cameras and marked the beginning of a lifetime fascination with photographing pure road racing that is celebrated in these pages.

When Clifford captured his Cloughwater picture in the mid-sixties I was just five years old. By the time I got my hands on a camera and was shooting Robert Dunlop from the same spot in 1987, both motorcycle road racing and photography had changed a great deal.

Clifford enjoyed the privilege of shooting the best riders on the planet at the Isle of Man TT and the Ulster Grand Prix at a time when both venues still hosted rounds of the Grand Prix world championship. He documented the shift in the sport as new, homegrown talents such as Tom Herron, Joey Dunlop and the rest of the Armoy Armada took on the best international riders on closed roads.

Stephen Davison at Mountain Box on the Isle of Man TT course in 2006.

With his completely manual Leica and Nikon cameras loaded with black and white film and a small smattering of colour transparency stock, Clifford recorded all the action on the local circuits. Film was an expensive medium, only offering a maximum of thirty-six shots per roll, and the high costs of processing often limited him to five or six rolls per meeting. He was forced to be very precise with his focussing and exposure, something that was far from easy as he attempted to capture motorcycles travelling at over 100mph in ever-changing light. His unerring ability to do so is documented in his images that are reproduced in the first three sections of this book.

Although I also shot film for several years, by the time I started to work as a professional photographer in the nineties the digital revolution was beginning in photography. Cameras had already made quantum improvements with better metering and autofocus systems and digital brought new benefits. These changes mean that many of the limitations that faced Clifford are no longer a factor for me. These days, as soon as an image is captured it is possible to see immediately whether it has turned out as you had hoped. Where once Clifford shot less than two

MV Agusta rider Phil Read after winning the 1974 Mallory Park Race of the Year. Clifford McLean is on the left in the background.

hundred frames over the whole weekend of the North West 200, I can now shoot many thousands with no extra expense in consumables. Although there is still only one chance to capture the moment, success is no longer such a mystery and failure is not as expensive as it once was.

Such change brings new pressures. Where Clifford's involvement with his pictures and their publication largely ended at the point of capture, nowadays I use the very latest technology to send my images from the hedgerow within seconds of shooting them. Deadlines shorten as the ability to meet them improves. Time once spent in the darkroom is now passed in front of a computer screen.

Although we have used different equipment and methods to record the sport through changing eras both Clifford and I have come to the sport by the same route. For both of us our road racing photography was the coalescence of two great loves – photography and motorcycles. And our objective has always been the same – the thrill of capturing a wonderful moment forever.

As it does for the racers, road racing offers a unique challenge to every photographer. Equipment for

Clifford McLean pictured at the Glenmanus Reformed Presbyterian Church in Portrush. Clifford is an elder of the church and he has photographed from its grounds at every North West 200 for over forty years.

Stephen Davison photographs Ryan Farquhar (KMR Kawasaki) at Tournagrough during the 2010 Ulster Grand Prix.

both riders and photographers is very expensive with a very poor return, both for the amount of money invested and for the huge amount of time spent in preparation, travel and participation. Competition in both disciplines is fierce with experience and course knowledge providing the keys to progress for rider and photographer alike. Every course is driven and walked beforehand, each corner considered from every angle. Just as a racer maps the racing line and commits it to memory, so too does the photographer. A vantage point just a few feet to the left or right at any location can make or break a photograph.

Each race meeting is run under different weather conditions at different venues and the successful rider and photographer must have the ability to adapt quickly to constantly changing circumstances. For everyone involved, everything that happens in racing does so at an incredible speed. The person who will triumph from either side of the hedge will be the one who can bring every element of their

Stephen Davison's first road racing photograph – Robert Dunlop on the Dundee Autos 250 at Cloughwater Church corner during the 1987 Mid-Antrim 150

game together to make the right decisions under intense pressure.

As little as possible is left to chance but luck will always play an important role in any type of action sport or photography. Clifford and I and every rider I have ever met would be quick to recognise the part played by this unquantifiable but essential element in what we do.

There is, of course, one huge difference between the challenge to the road racer and the road racing photographer – for the rider the consequences of error are much more serious. Crashes, injury and death are, sadly, part of the sport and covering such events raises issues for photographers. Both Clifford and I have had to photograph the funerals of friends who have lost their lives while racing. We know the families left behind, see their loss and feel their pain. This is an intrinsic part of the most dangerous sport in the world and we cannot turn away from it. We must do our job, we must tell the truth with the camera.

Every author fears writer's block, every painter or sculptor worries that their muse will desert them. But a writer can imagine a story and a painter can paint from a photograph or be stirred by an idea. They can all begin again from within. A photographer, however, must go out and physically engage with the world to capture images. There is no other way and every time we begin the camera is always empty.

A photograph cannot be imagined, it must be seen, and the photographer has to be there to do the seeing. The ground has to be covered.

Although luck will always have its say, it is also true that the harder you work the luckier you get. The more ground you cover with the camera, the more opportunities you have to capture something special. Of course, there is more to it than a simple law of averages. If you cannot see a picture, you will never be able to take a picture. This skill cannot be taught. There is something that must be felt when you look at a scene, something inside yourself that makes you feel the photograph. Chasing that feeling is what photography is all about.

Being involved in road racing with our cameras has been a great privilege for both Clifford and myself. We have travelled to many wonderful places, met very special people and enjoyed the pure pleasure of documenting all of this over many years. We have done a great many things that neither of us could ever have dreamed of doing when we first poked our lenses through those church railings.

And we aren't finished yet!

STEPHEN DAVISON

An early image from Clifford McLean's archive of Billy McCosh arriving for scrutineering with his 500cc Matchless at the garage at the back of the Carric-na-cule Hotel during the North West 200 in the mid-sixties

Brian Steenson (Aermacchi) leads
Bill Smith (Honda), 350cc race,
Henry's Corner, 1968.

North West 200

Given its current pre-eminence as the biggest Irish road racing event of the year, it is sometimes forgotten that until the 1990s the North West 200 did not hold such a significant position in the racing calendar. Never a scoring round of any major championship meant that the North West 200 was little more than a holiday race that presented an opportunity for riders to earn a few pounds early in the season. However, the seaside location and tireless efforts of the organising club have seen the North West's fortunes rise. As Clifford McLean's 'home' race, it has always held a special place in his affections but there is another important reason why he has so many fond memories of it.

'The 1967 North West 200 was the first race that I ever worked at as a photographer,' Clifford explains. 'Back then it was difficult to get a photographer's pass to shoot the races and I had tried to get one many times without success. In the winter of '67 I wrote to the editor of *Motorcycle News* and asked if he would be interested in me photographing the event for the paper. Amazingly he wrote back two weeks before the race and said yes and I was in!'

Armed with his road pass, Clifford could make his way around the circuit with privileged access and this honoured position gave him a feeling that is enjoyed by most photographers. 'I felt part of the event, I was on the inside. In those days there weren't that many photographers and I was over the moon to walk out onto the circuit with my pass.'

It was a far cry from his first visit as a four-year-old to the 1947 North West with his father. 'My father belonged to Ballymoney Motorcycle Club and each of the local clubs marshalled a section

9

of the course, so my father took me along,' Clifford recalls. 'We usually watched from either Henry's Corner in Portstewart or the Metropole at Portrush. There was a great build-up around the town on the week before the races and we would go to the little garage in Portstewart that was used for scrutineering to catch a glimpse of stars like Geoff Duke, Reg Armstrong, Bob McIntyre, Eric Hinton and Jack Brett as they arrived with their bikes.'

Memories were etched that would prove indelible. 'Even though I was only twelve at the time, I have never forgotten the sight and sound of Duke and Armstrong roaring around Henry's Corner on their Gileras in 1955.'

It would be another twelve years before Clifford would walk along Portstewart Promenade with his camera to capture the action. But almost immediately he was shooting exclusive images. In 1969 Phil Read brought a Westlake Twin machine to the North West that had cost hundreds of thousands of pounds to develop and was being heralded as a 'British world-beater'. Embarrassingly it only got as far as Henry's Corner on its opening practice session where Clifford was waiting with his Leica.

'I got a shot of Read on the Westlake and then it spluttered to a halt a few yards further along the prom, never to reappear again. It was the only picture of the Westlake in action and it appeared in a lot more places than that bike ever did,' Clifford laughs.

Tommy Robb

During the fifteen years that Clifford worked for *Motorcycle News* he never missed a North West. Although he was the local man on the ground with the inside track on the riders and the course, he is quick to acknowledge the vision of a fresh eye and the lessons that it can teach. 'Sometimes we think we have everything covered but I remember an English photographer called Malcolm Carling coming to the North West one year and he found a great place to shoot the race – at the opposite end of the promenade to where we usually took pictures. None of us had ever thought of it before.'

Phil Read on the Westlake, Henry's Corner, 1969

Clifford still shoots the North West 200 today, though he laments the restrictions that have been brought in over the years and that have made his job more difficult: 'Access to some of the best spots for pictures has become much more limited. The bikes are a lot faster now and safety concerns have led to more and more places becoming out of bounds. No one would argue against the need for this but it is frustrating because I still think about how many great pictures I could get if it was as free as it was in the old days.'

Ralph Bryans (250cc 6-cylinder Honda), Henry's Corner, 1968

The podium of the 1967 500cc North West 200 race.
L–R: Fred Stevens (1st), John Blanchard (2nd) and
Malcolm Uphill (3rd) with Miss North West 200.

The podium of the 1969
350cc North West 200 race.
Rod Gould (1st, centre),
Phil Read (2nd, left) and
Jack Findlay (3rd) with
Miss North West 200.

The podium of the 1974 250cc North West 200 race.
L–R: Ray McCullough (1st), John Williams (2nd), Mick Grant (3rd)
with Miss North West 200.

The 250cc field takes to the circuit for a wet evening practice in 1974; Mervyn Robinson (40), Billy Guthrie (14), Tony Rutter (1), John Williams (2), Tom Herron (8), Phil Carpenter (17) and Barry Randel (5) make up the front row.

Charlie Williams (4) and Mick Grant (23), both on Yamahas, at the start of the 350cc race, 1974

Tony Rutter (4) leads Ian Richards (25), Noel Hudson (15) and Ray McCullough (1), all on Yamahas, into Church Corner past the railway embankment at Metropole, 250cc race,1977.

Kel Carruthers leads Phil Read (Yamaha) into Portstewart during the 1969 North West 200.

Ron Haslam, 1979

Percy Tait and
Stan Woods, 1976

FAR LEFT: Paul Smart warms up
his 350cc Yamaha, 1971.

LEFT: Steve Parrish prepares his 750cc
Yamaha in the paddock, 1981.

Barry Ditchburn and Mick Grant (both on Kawasakis) at Metropole Corner in the 1975 North West 200

The Honda Britain team sets up camp in the paddock in 1982 on what is now the start and finish chicane of the North West 200 racing circuit. The riders in the team were Ron Haslam, Wayne Gardner and Joey Dunlop.

Joey Dunlop (750 RFV Honda) at Metropole, 1987

Robert Dunlop (4) leads Ian Lougher (1) and
Brian Reid (2), all on Yamahas, into Church
Corner during the 250cc race, 1991.

Brian Reid leads Derek Young, Ian Duffus and Jonny Rea
at Ballysally roundabout in the 400cc Race, 1993.

Giacomo Agostini (MV Agusta) at Tournagrough in the 1968 350cc race

The Prix

The Ulster Grand Prix has been run on two courses during its history. For the first thirty years of its life, from 1922 until 1952, it was run over the Clady course that included the famous Seven Mile Straight section. From 1953 until the present the Ulster has used the shorter but blisteringly fast Dundrod circuit. Clifford McLean has watched the race at both venues.

The McLean family often watched the high-speed action from a wall at Clady corner, the turn at the end of the fearsomely fast seven-mile-long straight which tortured the tyres of the day. 'My father had a piece of rubber that had flown off Serafini's tyre when he won the Grand Prix in 1939 on a Gilera,' Clifford remembers. 'It was in the house for years.'

As a photographer Clifford was lucky enough to cover the last few years of the Ulster as a world championship round at Dundrod. All of the stars of the Grand Prix circus competed there, until the race lost its world championship status in 1971.

'In spite of the grey Dundrod skies that almost always brought rain, the Ulster was much more exotic and glamorous than any other race that I covered,' Clifford recalls. 'Even the names of the machines – MV Agusta, Benelli, Jamathi, MZ – had a mystique about them. It was wonderful to have the chance to see all of the big names in motorbike racing like Hailwood, Redman, Read and Ivy on our home patch but for me the highlight of these years was meeting and photographing Agostini. He had so much presence and charisma, I was totally in awe of him.'

It is not surprising that Clifford was so impressed by the Italian genius who would eventually win fifteen world championships. 'I could never quite get over the fact that he was speaking to me and letting me take his picture, asking me if it was working out okay.' But Clifford was not so much in awe of Agostini that he didn't capture some of the finest portraits ever taken of the Italian legend, the most successful motorcycle racer of all time.

Once again Clifford's status as a *Motorcycle News* photographer helped open doors to opportunities that would otherwise have been denied to him. 'In the sixties you needed a police pass to be allowed to take a vehicle onto the roads on the inside of the

The 500cc Ulster Grand Prix grid in 1970. Giacomo Agostini (2) leads away Christian Ravel (33), Jack Findlay (1), Percy Tait (19), Peter Williams (10), Malcolm Uphill (7), Ginger Molloy (56), Theo Louwes (46), Ron Chandler (29) and Tommy Robb (20).

Giacomo Agostini takes his 500cc MV Agusta to scrutineering during the 1969 Ulster Grand Prix.

circuit and I was able to get one of these because I was accredited to the paper,' Clifford says. 'That meant I was able to get around the course using the inner access roads which allowed me to cover many more places. Everything was so much more tightly controlled in those days, especially at a premier event like the Grand Prix.'

The huge profile of the event in the late sixties and early seventies increased the pressure on the photographer as well and Clifford had to be certain to use his exclusive access to capture award-winning images. 'Our films would be collected at the end of the day's racing by the journalists who would take them back to the paper's offices in Kettering on the next plane out of Aldergrove.'

Incredibly, this meant that Clifford had no idea what any of his pictures had turned out like until *Motorcycle News* was published the following Wednesday. 'We didn't get to develop our own films so we had to wait until we saw the paper. I couldn't sleep at night wondering how it would all turn out. I could hardly wait for Wednesday morning!'

During his fifteen years working as a road racing photographer for *Motorcycle News* and later for *Motorcyclist Illustrated*, Clifford produced dozens of brilliant images of the Ulster. Seeing his work in print was a huge thrill. 'Getting a picture on the front page was the biggest buzz of all and if you did you would leave the paper lying around on the desk at work so that everyone could see it!' he laughs.

Giacomo Agostini on the grid at the 1970 Ulster Grand Prix

Dick Creith smiling after finishing second to Phil Read in the 1964 500cc Ulster Grand Prix

Phil Read and Bill Ivy (both on Yamahas) at Cochranstown during the 1968 125cc Ulster Grand Prix

Heinz Rosner (MZ) at the Hairpin in the 1968 250cc Ulster Grand Prix

Barry Smith (Derrbi) at Leathemstown in the 1970 50cc Ulster Grand Prix

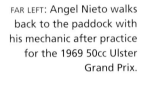

FAR LEFT: Angel Nieto walks back to the paddock with his mechanic after practice for the 1969 50cc Ulster Grand Prix.

LEFT: Honda mechanics wheel two 250cc 6-cylinder Hondas through the paddock to scrutineering during the 1967 Ulster Grand Prix. These machines were to be ridden by Mike Hailwood and Ralph Bryans.

Barry Sheene never competed at
Dundrod, but he rode a 125cc Suzuki in
the 1972 Ulster Grand Prix, which was
held at Bishopscourt that year during a
time of civil unrest in Northern Ireland.

Ray McCullough (1) follows Tom Herron (31),
both on Yamahas, around the Hairpin during
the 350cc race at the 1975 Ulster Grand Prix.

The start of the 250cc race at the 1975 Ulster Grand Prix. Ray McCullough (1), John Weedon (27), Eddie Roberts (8), Abe Alexander (6), Tom Herron (31), Derek Chatterton (4), Neil Tuxworth (7), and Tony Rutter (2) form the front row.

BELOW: John Williams on the podium after his win in the 500cc class of the 1978 Ulster Grand Prix. Later in the day Williams crashed in the 1000cc race at Wheeler's Corner, and died in hospital that evening.

ABOVE: Stan Woods (1st) and Joey Dunlop (2nd) on the podium after the 500cc race at the 1976 Ulster Grand Prix

LEFT: Team boss Hector Neill and Joey Dunlop stand beside the Neill Suzuki (40) as Tom Herron sits on the Finlay Suzuki (1) on the grid of the 500cc race at the 1978 Ulster Grand Prix.

John Newbold (14, Suzuki) leads Ron Haslam (2, Honda), Mick Grant (10, Honda) and Graham Crosby (12, Suzuki) at Leathemstown in the TT Formula One race at the 1980 Ulster Grand Prix.

BUSH
BRIDGE

The Armoy Armada at the Bush river
bridge in Armoy in the1970s – Jim
Dunlop, Frank Kennedy, Joey Dunlop
and Mervyn Robinson

Armoy Armada

Hailing from the same area of County Antrim and knowing some of the riders personally placed Clifford McLean in pole position to document the exploits of the legendary Armoy Armada in the mid-seventies.

'Frank Kennedy worked as a mechanic in a garage in Ballymoney. I would meet him on the street and we would talk about the racing,' Clifford remembers. 'I bumped into him one day and he was all bandaged up with a dislocated shoulder and his arm in a sling but all he was talking about was getting the bandages off and going racing the next weekend.'

Frank was one of four racers from the Armoy/Ballymoney area in County Antrim who came to be known as the 'Armoy Armada'. Mervyn Robinson and the Dunlop brothers, Joey and Jim, made up the rest of the foursome that was made famous by David Wallace's brilliant documentary *The Road Racers*, filmed in the late seventies. Wallace captured brilliantly the mood and atmosphere as the racers took part in illegal test sessions on open public roads around the little County Antrim village of Armoy and late-night spannering sessions in the Kennedy garage.

To some extent the film (which was not broadcast until some time later) and the subsequent tragic fate of the Armada created a legend that was not immediately apparent at the time. 'Although I knew all of the boys we weren't really aware of any kind of group or team,' Clifford explains. 'The whole Armoy Armada thing was really a supporters club that was aimed at raising money to go racing but when the boys went racing they did so as individuals, trying to beat each other every bit as much as the rest of the racers. They were all great characters and I always tried to get pictures of them at the races. I would sometimes have been out at Frank's garage at night in Armoy where the boys worked at their bikes between races and I know now I should have tried to capture more of what went on behind the scenes. We never thought that things would turn out the way they did and I only realised later how special a time it was. It is my greatest regret in photography that I didn't capture more of that time.'

Frank Kennedy (Sparton) at Metropole Corner in the
500cc race at the 1976 North West 200

Frank Kennedy (Suzuki) on the grid at
the 1978 Ulster Grand Prix

Although he has still given us a unique photographic record of the Armoy Armada, Clifford would not be alone amongst photographers in feeling this way about missed opportunities. We all have regrets about pictures that got away, things that we wish we had shot but didn't. There are often a million reasons not to take photographs – the weather is bad, you are in a hurry to get somewhere, the cameras are all packed away in the bag for the day and so on – but as soon as you go past something it always nags in the back of your mind that someday you will regret not taking that moment longer to stop and take a simple picture.

Although Clifford didn't photograph the quartet very much away from the races, he took great pride in seeing them winning on the track. 'I know that as a press man I should have been impartial but I was totally biased – I wanted Joey and Big Frank and the rest of the boys from home to win every race!' he laughs.

The Armada's sternest competition came from Ray McCullough, Brian Reid and Trevor Steele, a trio of County Down racers who became known as the 'Dromara Destroyers'. 'The battles between Ray and Joey in particular were really intense,' Clifford recalls. 'Ray was the kingpin of Irish road racing at the time. He worked in the Mechanical Engineering Department at Queen's University in Belfast and had race support from the department. Joey was the up-and-coming young fellow with very little money and riding rough and ready bikes. He was very much the underdog and I always back the underdog.'

Joey did, of course, succeed, and in a way that no one then could ever have imagined. But it came at a high cost. In 1979, Joey and Clifford lost their good friend Frank Kennedy following a crash at the North West 200.

Mervyn Robinson (Yamaha) at Tournagrough on his way
to victory in the 1975 500cc race at the Ulster Grand Prix

Mervyn Robinson on the grid of the 1975 500cc race
at the Ulster Grand Prix

'I walked past the scene of Frank's accident on the Cromore road after the race and his bike was still lying there in bits,' Clifford remembers. 'It was an awful sight. Frank was such a jovial character, full of life and fun.'

A year later, Mervyn Robinson lost his life in a crash at the same race and the Armoy Armada was disbanded. For a time it seemed that racing would end completely for the Dunlop brothers but they decided to go on, Jim for a few more years and Joey for another two decades until he lost his life in a crash in Estonia in 2000.

Joey's success with Honda in the Formula One World Championships at the start of the eighties brought him fame and much media attention and once again Clifford was well placed to record the fortunes of his fellow Ballymoney man.

'Joey was really in demand through those years and I was taking his picture all the time,' Clifford says. 'If I needed a picture it was never a problem, I would call up at his house and he would wheel out a bike or pull on his leathers for the shot. We even had a wee business deal together where I would get prints made, Joey would sign them and we would split the proceeds of the sales.'

Joey Dunlop (left) with the other members of the
legendary Armoy Armada – Frank Kennedy, Jim Dunlop
and Mervyn Robinson – outside the village of Armoy

Mervyn Robinson celebrates winning the 500cc race at the 1975 Ulster Grand Prix.

Perhaps remembering the missed opportunities with the Armoy quartet, Clifford stayed close to Joey with his camera throughout the following years, documenting events in and around their County Antrim home town.

'I photographed Joey's receipt of the award of the Freedom of the Borough of Ballymoney and I was also at the reception given in his honour after he returned from the TT in 2000, just a couple of weeks before his death.'

Mervyn Robinson (22) leads Joey Dunlop (34) and Neil Tuxworth (7), all on Yamahas, at Tournagrough during the 1976 Ulster Grand Prix.

Jim Dunlop (Yamsel) at Wheeler's Corner at the
Ulster Grand Prix in the 1970s

Jim and Joey Dunlop at the
North West 200 in the 1970s

Joey Dunlop (right) and
Noel Hudson with their
garlands after victories at
52   the 1975 Tandragee 100

Joey Dunlop (Yamaha) at
the 1978 Mid-Antrim 150

Ray McCullough receives the trophy after winning the 350cc race at the 1976
Ulster Grand Prix. Ian Richards (left) was second and John Weedon third.

RIGHT: Trevor Steele (Yamaha) at Metropole Corner at the North West 200

Brian Reid (EMC) at Metropole in the 250cc race
at the 1987 North West 200

Joey with a broken exhaust on the Rea Racing Yamaha
at Metropole, NW 200, 1977

Ray McCullough on the immaculate Irish Racing
Motorcycles Yamaha at the Tandragee 100, 1978

Joey Dunlop, 1982

Joey in the paddock at the
1988 North West 200

Joey on the grid at the
1981 North West 200

Joey in the paddock at the 1988 North
West 200

Joey riding for Suzuki at the
1980 Ulster Grand Prix

In June 2000 Clifford captured perhaps the saddest image of his career, the last photograph of Joey Dunlop with his family. 'Joey was my favourite racer of all the riders I have seen and met, he was one of our own and I was really lucky and privileged to have had the time and access to photograph him the way that I did. That has been the highlight of my photographic career.'

The last photograph taken of Joey Dunlop in public with his family outside his pub on a night of celebration in Ballymoney to mark his twenty-sixth Isle of Man TT win just a few days before he left for Estonia in June 2000. Joey is pictured with his wife Linda and children Donna, Gary, Joanne, Richard and Julie.

The next generation

The Dunlop dynasty is the royal family of road racing. Forty years ago Clifford McLean began photographing Joey and Jim Dunlop and a few years later their younger brother, Robert. I also enjoyed many happy days recording their exploits. The racing achievements of this Ballymoney clan are colossal and well documented in words and pictures. Sadly, Jim is the only surviving member of the trio but the legacy lives on in a new generation of Dunlop racers; Sam, the son of Jim, and William and Michael, the sons of Robert.

Still all in their early twenties, the three youngsters have inherited the family's skill for speed and have already amassed a successful portfolio in the sport. Irish National, Manx Grand Prix, Scarborough, North West 200, Ulster Grand Prix and Isle of Man TT wins are all already listed under the cousins' names in the record books. They are DNA'd winners, bringing them much attention and a huge following.

Like the generation that preceded them, it is not just what they have won but the manner of their triumphs that has caught the public's attention. Dry humour and self-effacing remarks are coupled with a style and power on the race track that has helped them handle the pressures of being the sons of famous fathers.

Although their uncle Joey was an inspiration, much of what they know of racing they learnt from Robert and Jim. Jim retired from the sport in the 1980s but he is still constantly at the side of his son and nephews in the paddock. On the track, Robert mentored the juniors in racing lines and tactics.

William Dunlop (6) leads his brother Michael (3), both on Hondas, 250cc race, Skerries, July 2008

Robert Dunlop with his two sons Michael and William, Belfast Motorcycle Show, 2002

Robert with his son William and nephew Sam, Skerries, July 2005

Media attention is focussed on the young Dunlops wherever they go. As Clifford did all those years ago with their fathers, I have been documenting the rise of the new Dunlop generation, from their earliest race meetings to international road race success. Full of fun and mischief, the boys are always willing to help with a picture, no matter when or where I ask.

Fascinating to watch and be around both on and off the bikes, they, like Joey and Robert, simply get on with their work and ignore the camera. One of my greatest pleasures in making motorcycle racing images was sitting quietly with the camera, occasionally taking a picture as Joey or Robert worked on their bikes with a quiet intensity that allowed them to shut out everything around them.

Much of what I see through my camera today harks back to halcyon days, providing a sense of continuity in a family and a sport that has been fractured by loss.

William, Michael and Sam exhibit many of the personality traits found in all three of the senior Dunlops and, although they are their own men, they are fiercely determined to uphold the proud tradition of their dynasty.

Robert Dunlop (4) and his son William (6),
both on Hondas, Kells, July 2004

Robert Dunlop (4, Aprilia) and his nephew
Sam (33, Honda), Kells, July 2004

Sam Dunlop and his father Jim,
Cookstown 100, April 2009

William Dunlop on his way to victory
ahead of Davy Morgan (both on Hondas)
in the 250cc race, Armoy, August 2010

67

Sam Dunlop (Honda), Spademill Jump,
Bush, June 2009

69

Michael Dunlop (Crossan Suzuki),
Hanlon's Leap, Kells, July 2008

Michael Dunlop celebrates winning the Supersport
TT, his first TT victory, Isle of Man, June 2009.

Michael Dunlop (Street Sweep Yamaha) at
the Dark Hedges, Stranocum, May 2009

William Dunlop at his Ballymoney home, January 2010

William Dunlop (Flynn Honda), Black's Farm,
Cookstown 100, April 2009

Sam, on the bike, with William and Gary Dunlop, Clubman's meeting, Nutt's Corner, April 2001. Gary, who raced for several seasons before retiring, is the son of Joey Dunlop.

Sam Dunlop (Honda), 125cc race, Killalane, September 2009

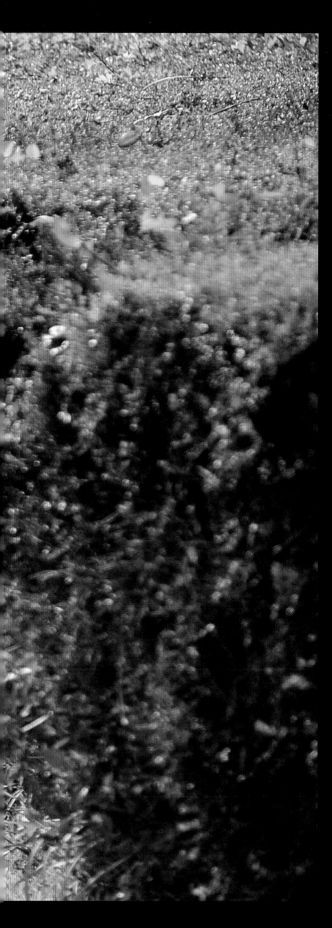

Michael Dunlop (Street Sweep Yamaha),
Mackney's Corner, Cookstown 100, April 2009

Scarborough

During the course of every race I meet dozens of people I know – riders, officials, race fans, fellow photographers – and I often think that it would be great to be able to stop and have a chat, catch up on news and maybe share a cup of tea here and there. But usually I can manage little more than a quick hello because once the racing has begun I am on a mission to capture as much of the day's action, of every kind, as I can. I often feel guilty that everything else is set aside in pursuit of trying to capture these moments.

Every race meeting is approached like a military operation. There has to be a plan of attack. If a course is new to me I drive around it, at least several times, before walking the sections that I think will be the most interesting photographically. Scarborough's Oliver's Mount parkland circuit is home to the only road race on closed public roads in England. On my first photographic foray to the Yorkshire venue Ryan Farquhar walked me round a full lap, showing me the spots where he wheelied or brushed the hedges. I always want to find those places where the riders are most commited.

This, though, is only one aspect of my approach. Working for a variety of press outlets means that I must supply images of the whole event, so I have to cover everything, from race starts to podiums, as well as any newsworthy stories or incidents I come across during the day. Course knowledge and the schedule of the meeting must dovetail together into an overall plan that will involve constantly shifting location.

William Dunlop takes the chequered flag ahead of Ian Lougher (both on Hondas) to win the 125cc race, Scarborough Gold Cup, September 2009.

This is a little bit easier to manage at the enclosed Scarborough circuit than it would be at an Irish road race and a whole lot easier than it is on the TT's Mountain course. But it still means ascending the steep slopes of the parkland course several times during every meeting with 30lb of camera kit!

ABOVE: Ryan Farquhar and Guy Martin, Scarborough Gold Cup, September 2008

LEFT: Ryan Farquhar (KMR Kawasaki) leads Ian Hutchinson (Padgett's Honda) and Guy Martin (Hydrex Honda), Memorial Bends, Scarborough Gold Cup, September 2009.

John McGuinness (Padgett's Honda), Jefferies Jumps,
Scarborough Gold Cup, September 2008

Ian Lougher (2) and William Dunlop (6), both on Hondas, Memorial
Bends, Scarborough Gold Cup, September 2008

Ultimately there are two aims. One is to come away from any
race with a good variety of images and the other is that some
of those images will be shots that I have never captured
before. Often taking the picture is the easy part of the job – it
is finding out where and when something will happen that is
the tricky part. Armed with that knowledge everything else
falls into place.

85

These images from Scarborough, taken over the last couple of Gold Cup meetings, are a small selection of perhaps a hundred pictures that are included in an edit from each event. I like to show the men behind the helmets in my photographs and I love to try to capture some sense of the wonderful places where they race. Often the motorbike is almost incidental in these pictures as I work out the angle and then wait for a bike to appear just where I want it to be to make the shot.

I always laugh when people tell me that photography is just about standing there and going 'click'! A great deal of planning goes into every assignment. There are pictures everywhere – on my way up the slope, I noticed a patch of early morning light filtering down through the trees as I crossed a bridge at Mountside; listening to the general chat around the grid I discovered that Ryan Farquhar needed a painkilling injection to be able to race; and as I headed back to the podium I noticed Guy Martin's parents in the paddock, waiting to join him for a post-race celebratory beer.

So that is why I never have any time to stop to chat. I will still always feel guilty about running on past but I am not being rude, it's just that I am scared of missing something if I don't keep on the move!

Guy Martin (Hydrex Honda), Mick Goodings (Yamaha) and Ryan Farquhar (KMR Kawasaki), Mountside, Scarborough Gold Cup, September 2008

John McGuinness
(Padgett's Honda),
Bottom Straight,
Scarborough Gold
Cup, September
2008

Michael Dunlop (Street Sweep Yamaha) drifting into Mere Hairpin,
Supersport race, Scarborough Gold Cup, September 2010

Ryan Farquhar (KMR Kawasaki), Mere
Hairpin, Scarborough Spring Cup, April 2009

Ryan Farquhar receives a painkilling injection in his
wrist, Scarborough Gold Cup, September 2009.

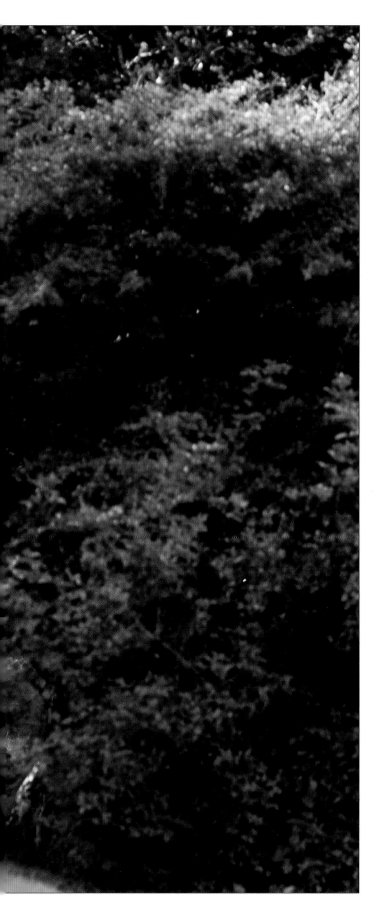

Guy Martin enjoys a celebratory drink with his
parents, Rita and Ian, after winning the Scarborough
Gold, September 2008.

Guy Martin (Hydrex Honda), Scarborough
Gold Cup, September 2008

TT

Although the Isle of Man TT race festival has many attractions it is, above all else, about one thing; the infamous Mountain course. A 37³/₄-mile-long tarmac ribbon that sweeps through towns and villages, glens and mountains, forests and moors in its unrelenting passage from the sea's edge in Douglas to the heights of Snaefell.

From minute to minute and lap by lap the course can change as rain falls on Ramsey but not in Kirkmichael, as mist swirls around the Verandah to dull the blazing sun that still shines on Kate's Cottage further below. From season to season the winter frosts and humdrum passage of traffic disturb the road surface and shift the camber, altering the racing line.

The course is an organic, living being, ever-changing, ever-challenging and always ready to catch out those who do not know its ways. It is this that makes the TT the ultimate test of man and machine and in the first decade of the twenty-first century it has become a trial reborn.

The TT is more exciting to watch and photograph today than at any time in its history. The unique course is a picture factory for people like myself, offering thousands of vantage points to capture eye-searing action against stunningly beautiful landscapes. There is always somewhere new to go and the riders today are faster than ever before.

Just as it is for the racers, the course is also the greatest challenge in motorcycling for image-makers. The logistics of covering a race around this huge circuit are immensely difficult. It is not made any easier by the fact that in over one hundred years of racing, the powers-that-be have never constructed a proper traffic-carrying road or bridge that goes from the inside of the course to the outside once the roads are closed.

Gary Johnson (Robinson Honda), Rhencullen, Isle of Man TT, 2009

Negotiating my way along ramblers' footpaths and green lanes, through culverts beneath roads and over the hedges of residents' gardens (with their permission) becomes part of a typical fortnight of shooting the TT. Over time you learn the lie of the land.

All of this information is carefully stored and closely guarded – it can mean the difference between getting a great shot and just grabbing a mediocre one. And, of course, it can also ensure that you are the only photographer to get that winning shot if your rivals haven't unravelled the mystery of how to get to the right spot!

ABOVE: John McGuinness (HM Plant Honda), Mountain Box, Isle of Man TT, May 2006

LEFT: John McGuinness with a replica of his 2007 Senior TT winning HM Plant Honda. The bike, on which he also set the first ever 130mph plus lap of the Isle of Man Mountain course, sits under the stairs of his Morecambe home.

Ian Hutchinson (Padgett's Honda) crosses the finishing line to celebrate victory in the Senior TT and a record of five TT wins in one week, Isle of Man TT, June 2010.

Once the action has been captured it is back into the car or onto a bike to begin the journey back to the podium. As the battle rages on the race track, another battle against time and traffic is being fought along the Manx byways as I race back to the Grandstand for the podium celebrations.

Sometimes the drive can be ten or fifteen miles long, before the vehicle is abandoned at the back gate of the cemetery on Glencrutchry road. A quick sprint through the graveyard brings you to the front gates and climbing over these drops you down to the front of the famous lapboard from where you can shoot winner after winner taking the chequered flag. Then it's back over the cemetery railings and onto the footbridge into Nobles Park to get to the winners' enclosure and podium for the champagne and smiles.

Ian Hutchinson (Padgett's Honda), Tower Bends,
Superstock TT, Isle of Man TT, June 2010

With eight races in a week this ritual has to be repeated on a daily basis. Different plans have to be worked out for each race day so that you don't end up shooting the same pictures every time. By the end of the Senior TT, the final event of the festival, the ferry home can look very inviting!

For me, though, it is a labour of love. The setting of my 'factory' is magnificent and the elation of seeing 200mph race bikes tearing through it makes me feel more alive than anything else I know. The racing men who perform these feats are the most down-to-earth and accessible sportsmen you could imagine, especially when you consider what they put on the line to race on the island.

The TT is an event steeped in legend and memory and is very conscious of its long and illustrious history. In capturing one of those special moments you always hope that you are, in some small way, adding to the legend.

Keith Amor (Craig Honda), bottom of
Barregarrow, Isle of Man TT, June 2009

Steve Plater celebrates his first TT podium, Supersport TT, Isle of Man TT, June 2008.

Bruce Anstey celebrates
winning the Supersport TT,
Isle of Man TT, June 2008.

Spectators watch the evening practice action from the
Raven Pub at Ballaugh village, Isle of Man TT, 2007.

Guy Martin dons period costume to have some fun with (left to right) Richard Britton, Adrian Archibald, Ryan Farquhar and John McGuinness at the Isle of Man TT press launch, Creg Ny Baa, April 2005.

Guy Martin (AIM Yamaha), Guthries Bends, Isle of Man TT, May 2006

Conor Cummins (McAdoo Kawasaki),
Ballaugh Bridge, Isle of Man TT,
June 2010

A new golden era

The first decade of the twenty-first century has seen a wonderful resurgence in racing between the hedges of the Emerald Isle. Television coverage of the International North West 200 and Ulster Grand Prix events have raised the sport's profile and lured the big teams and their high-profile riders like Steve Plater, John McGuinness, Michael Rutter, Ian Lougher, Keith Amor, Conor Cummins, Guy Martin, Cameron Donald and Bruce Anstey onto the Irish roads. A new generation of Irish riders like Adrian Archibald, Ryan Farquhar and the young Dunlops have risen to the challenge of defending local honour against the visitors' onslaught.

While the larger events attract most of the fans' attention and media interest, the smaller National road racing scene has also been boosted by the renewed enthusiasm for the sport. New (or revived) races have appeared in places like Bush and Faugheen, Dunmanway and Walderstown, giving photographers the chance to shoot racing action every weekend from April until September.

The North West 200 and the Ulster Grand Prix are the 'big' days in Ireland, offering the chance of the most lucrative and prestigious wins. The Ulster Grand Prix is now the quickest course in the world, with an average lap speed of over 133mph, and everyone wants to hold the title of the 'fastest motorcycle racer in the world'. It is the cachet of these events that brings the photographer commissions from magazines and newspapers, the work that helps to pay the bills.

Ryan Farquhar (KMR Kawasaki),
Turnarobert, Armoy, August 2009

Bruce Anstey (TAS Suzuki), Quarry Bends,
Ulster Grand Prix, August 2005

Everything, and everyone, is at their peak on these big occasions and, as a photographer, you have to rise to the challenge. All of your experience and knowledge of the sport is brought into play and a reliable contact with a small piece of information can help you to get something that little bit dfferent. A tip-off from a friend in television provided me with the opportunity to shoot Steve Plater at the Giant's Causeway in 2009. Road racing photography, like road racing, is a highly competitive business and you have to attend to every small detail to win.

Michael Rutter (NW 200 Ducati) and Steve Plater
(AIM Yamaha) Millbank, North West 200, May 2008

While it is great to immerse yourself in all of the razzamatazz of the glitzier races, it is at the smaller National races where my heart really lies. These were the first races I ever attended as a youngster and they are run on quieter days, when there is more time to stop and pass the time of day with fellow racegoers as I move around the course.

There is no rush back to the podium – usually podiums are only held at the completion of the day's racing – and the race schedule is more relaxed. It is easier to get closer to the riders away from the high pressure of the International events.

On these kinds of days you have time to notice the little things that make these events uniquely Irish – the garage set up beside the telephone box, the team awning alongside the heap of manure in the paddock.

None of this means that the action is any less spectacular on the track. Races like Armoy or Tandragee are run on much narrower and bumpier roads than the smooth surfaces of the International meetings. Bumps mean jumps, sometimes even in the middle of corners, and like the racers, the photographer has to find these places.

For me, photographing motorbike racing has never really been about the motorbikes. Some of the machines are beautifully built and sound wonderful but it is the people that ride them and where they race that have drawn me into the sport. Portraying where we race, a sense of place, is as important to me as the action.

And every year I return with my camera, looking for something I have never seen before, hoping to capture a moment in a split second that will make the rest of my year feel fulfilled.

Dan Kneen (Yamaha), Supersport race,
North West 200, May 2009

Steve Plater (HM Plant Honda), North West 200,
May 2009

ABOVE RIGHT: Cameron Donald (Relentless
Suzuki), North West 200, May 2009

Guy Martin (Hydrex Honda),
North West 200, May 2009

Steve Plater with the HM Plant Honda,
Giant's Causeway, May 2009

119

A tea break for two race fans, Cooley Hill,
Tandragee 100, May 2009

Open race start, Tandragee 100, May 2009

Brian McCormack (Honda) and
Damian Mulleady (Yamaha),
Gillies Leap, Skerries 100, July 2010

123

Adrian Archibald (AMA Suzuki) chases
Michael Dunlop (Street Sweep Yamaha)
during the Grand Final, Killalane,
September 2009.

Adrian Archibald wheels his AMA Suzuki through the
paddock to the start of practice at the Mid-Antrim 150,
Clough, July 2009.

Ryan Farquhar (KMR Kawasaki) takes the chequered flag to win his 120th Irish National road race and break Joey Dunlop's record of wins, Killalane, September 2009.

Race winner Ryan Farquhar (centre), runner-up Keith Amor (right) and third-placed Michael Dunlop, Grand Final podium, Kells, July 2008

Ryan Farquhar (KMR Kawasaki), Quarry Bends,
Ulster Grand Prix, August 2009

Robert Dunlop (4) leads Darran Lindsay (5), both on Hondas,
Quarry Bends, Dundrod 150, August 2008

Richard Britton (O'Kane Suzuki) and Martin Finnegan (Round Tower Yamaha), Gillies Leap, Skerries, July 2004

All four men lost their lives in racing crashes in recent years – Robert Dunlop at the North West 200 in 2008, Darran Lindsay at Killalane in 2006, Richard Britton at Ballybunion in 2005 and Martin Finnegan at Tandragee in 2008.

LEFT: Support race, Black's Farm,
Cookstown 100, April 2004

Darren Burns' bikes being prepared in a makeshift
paddock on the footpath, Main Street, Clough village,
Mid-Antrim 150, August 2003

Spectators, Skerries 100, July 2009

CD Racing team, Athea paddock, June 2009

Open race, Clough Hairpin, Mid-Antrim 150, August 2009 135

Gary Johnson (Robinson Honda),
Hanlon's Leap, Kells, July 2009

Cameron Donald (Robinson Honda), Kells, July 2006

Keith Amor (KBMG BMW), at the exit of Sam's Tunnel,
Grand Final, Skerries 100, July 2010

The Munster 100 road race was resurrected in County Cork in August 2010 after a break of eighteen years. Michael Dunlop (Street Sweep Yamaha) races past the local shops in Dunmanway village during the 600cc race.

RIGHT: Dean Harrison (McKinstry Kawasaki) races into Dunmanway village, County Cork, during the Support race at the Munster 100, August 2010.

FAR LEFT: Wayne Kennedy (Honda) on the streets of Dunmanway in County Cork during the Munster 100, August 2010

LEFT: Enjoying their first taste of road racing in Dunmanway

Ryan Farquhar (KMR Kawasaki), Cochranstown,
Ulster Grand Prix, August 2009

Ryan Farquhar (KMR Kawasaki) and
Keith Amor (Craig Honda) at Hanlon's Leap
in the 600cc race at Kells, July 2009

First published in 2010 by
Blackstaff Press, 4c Heron Wharf
Sydenham Business Park
Belfast BT3 9LE, Northern Ireland

Text © Stephen Davison, 2010

Photographs on pages 1–7
© Pacemaker Press International, 2010
Photographs on pages 8–61 by Clifford McLean
© Pacemaker Press International, 2010
Photographs on pages 62–144 by Stephen Davison
© Pacemaker Press International, 2010
All rights reserved

Design by Dunbar Design
Printed and bound by Rotolito Lombarda

A CIP catalogue record for this book is available
from the British Library

ISBN 978-0-85640-856-4

www.blackstaffpress.com
www.pacemakerpressintl.com